5755 3512

See Them Grow

TURTLE

by Debby Freeman

Consultant: Sara Viernum
Wildlife Biologist and Herpetologist
Cofounder of The Wandering Herpetologist

BEARPORT
PUBLISHING

New York, New York

Credits

Cover, © RyanCSlimakPhoto/iStock; Title Page, © StevenRussellSmithPhotos/Shutterstock; TOC, © Teri Virbickis/Shutterstock; 4–5, © Nancy Hixson/Shutterstock, © Madlen/Shutterstock, and © David Byron Keener/Shutterstock; 6–7, © Rob vanNostrand/iStock; 7L, © Stevenrussellsmithphotos/Dreamstime; 7R, © Michelle D. Milliman/Shutterstock; 8, © Dwight Kuhn; 9, © Rick & Nora Bowers/Alamy; 10–11, © Gerardo A. Cordero and Fredric J. Janzen, An Enhanced Developmental Staging Table for the Painted Turtle, Chrysemys picta (testudines: Emydidae)/Wiley Publishing; 12, © Gregory Synstelien; 13, © Dwight Kuhn; 14TR, © Fat Jackey/Shutterstock; 14B, © Dwight Kuhn; 15, © Dwight Kuhn; 16, © Larry Mishkar/Seapics; 17L, © Eric Isselee/Shutterstock; 17R, © iceprotector/Shutterstock; 18 (T to B), © GTibbetts/Shutterstock, © GTibbetts/Shutterstock, and © Gerald A. DeBoer/Shutterstock; 19, © Phyllis L. Brown; 20, © S and D and K Maslowski/FLPA/Minden Pictures; 21, © PaulReevesPhotography/iStock; 22, © Teri Virbickis/Shutterstock; 23 (T to B), © Dwight Kuhn, © Isselee/Dreamstime, © Rob vanNostrand/iStock, © Audrey Snider-Bell/Shutterstock, and © Dwight Kuhn; 24, © Gerald A. DeBoer/Shutterstock.

Publisher: Kenn Goin
Senior Editor: Joyce Tavolacci
Creative Director: Spencer Brinker
Design: Debrah Kaiser
Photo Researcher: Thomas Persano

Library of Congress Cataloging-in-Publication Data in process at time of publication (2017)
Library of Congress Control Number: 2016038813
ISBN-13: 978-1-68402-041-6

For more information, write to Bearport Publishing Company, Inc., 45 West 21st Street, Suite 3B, New York, New York 10010. Printed in the United States of America.

10 9 8 7 6 5 4 3 2 1

Contents

Turtle

The sun shines on a pond.

A painted turtle warms
its body on a rock.

It has a hard, bony shell
and colorful stripes.

How did it get that way?

Turtles, like snakes and lizards, are **reptiles**.

It's springtime.

A male painted turtle waves his claws at a female.

He swims up to the female.

Then the turtles dive underwater and **mate**.

After mating, eggs grow inside the female's body.

Male painted turtles have longer claws than females.

male
claw

female
claw

In a few weeks, the female climbs onto shore.

She looks for warm, wet sand to dig a hole.

The turtle lays up to 20 eggs inside the hole.

Turtle eggs are soft and leathery.

Then she covers her nest with sand and dirt.

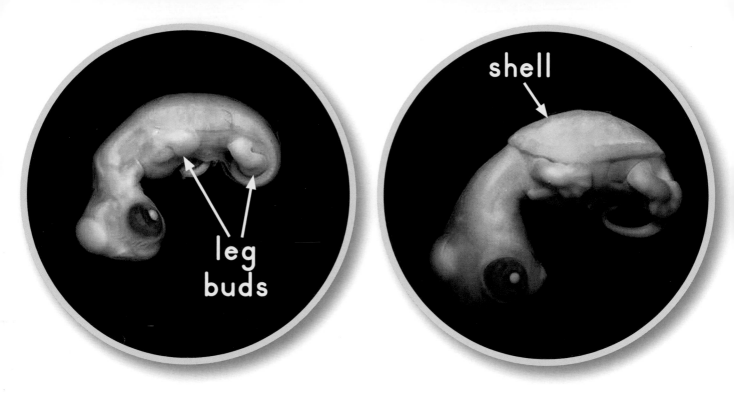

Inside each egg is a tiny **embryo.**

As the embryo grows, it changes.

If the nest is warmer than 84°F (29°C), the turtles will all be female. If it's cooler, the babies will all be male.

Leg buds form feet, toes, and claws.

A small round shell appears.

After about ten weeks, the baby turtle is ready to hatch.

Pip, pip, pip!

It uses a point on its **beak** to crack, or pip, its shell.

It can take hours—or days— for the baby to break free.

The pointed tip of the baby's beak is called an egg tooth.

The newly hatched turtle is about the size of a quarter.

It pushes through the dirt and sand.

Finally, it digs itself out of the nest.

Then the tiny hatchling races to the nearby pond.

yolk sac

Baby turtles are born with a pea-sized **yolk sac**. The yolk provides food for the babies for about a week.

Once in the water, the baby turtle looks for food.

It eats plants and small animals.

Painted turtles don't have teeth. They gulp water to help them swallow food.

Watch out! The tiny turtle has many enemies.

Raccoons and large birds try to eat it.

raccoon   heron

The baby turtle gets bigger and bigger.

As it grows, its shell grows too. How?

At night, the baby turtle sleeps in mud at the bottom of the pond. It can hold its breath for many hours.

The shell is covered with bony plates called scutes.

The old scutes fall off.

Then new, larger scutes grow in.

old scutes

After about a year, the painted turtle will have doubled in size.

It becomes an adult in three to eight years.

The turtle can live for more than 60 years!

Female turtles grow much larger than males.

Turtle Facts

❋ Painted turtles can be found throughout North America.

❋ There are four different kinds of painted turtles.

❋ In cold areas, painted turtles rest in thick mud at the bottom of ponds during winter.

❋ Turtles can escape from danger by peeing on their enemies!

Glossary

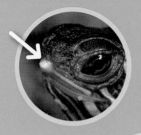
beak (BEEK) the hard, pointed part of a turtle's mouth

embryo (EM-bree-oh) an animal in the first stage of development

mate (MAYT) to come together to have young

reptiles (REP-tyelz) cold-blooded animals that have dry, scaly skin, such as turtles, alligators, and snakes

yolk sac (YOKE SAK) a small pouch that holds the part of an egg that feeds the embryo

Index

Read More

Chrustowski, Rick. *Turtle Crossing.* New York: Henry Holt (2006).

Hipp, Andrew. *The Life Cycle of a Painted Turtle.* New York: Rosen (2002).

Learn More Online

To learn more about turtles, visit

www.bearportpublishing.com/SeeThemGrow

About the Author

Debby Freeman lives with her two daughters, Amy and Cassidy, near Turtleback Park. They like to paint pictures of turtles.